Recipes

No.	Description	Starters	Soups	Salads	Main courses	Desserts	Bread	Biscuits	Drinks
1	Mini Doughnuts							██	
2	Chocolate Brownies							██	
3									
4									
5									
6									
7									
8									
9									
10									
11									
12									
13									
14									
15									
16									
17									
18									
19									
20									
21									
22									
23									
24									
25									

No.	Description	Starters	Soups	Salads	Main courses	Desserts	Bread and cakes	Biscuits and snacks	Drinks
26									
27									
28									
29									
30									
31									
32									
33									
34									
35									
36									
37									
38									
39									
40									
41									
42									
43									
44									
45									
46									
47									
48									
49									
50									

No.	Description	Starters	Soups	Salads	Main courses	Desserts	Bread and cakes	Biscuits and snacks	Drinks
51									
52									
53									
54									
55									
56									
57									
58									
59									
60									
61									
62									
63									
64									
65									
66									
67									
68									
69									
70									
71									
72									
73									
74									
75									

No.	Description	Starters	Soups	Salads	Main courses	Desserts	Bread and cakes	Biscuits and snacks	Drinks
76									
77									
78									
79									
80									
81									
82									
83									
84									
85									
86									
87									
88									
89									
90									
91									
92									
93									
94									
95									
96									
97									
98									
99									
100									

Recipe:

3

Ingredients:

Method:

Notes:

Serves:

🕐 Preparation time:

🕐 Cooking time:

Suitable for freezing: Y / N

Calories per serving:

Difficulty?
1 2 3 4 5

How healthy?
1 2 3 4 5

Date first made:

Taste test:

Recipe:

4

Ingredients:

_____   _____
_____   _____
_____   _____
_____

Serves:

⏲ Preparation time:

⏲ Cooking time:

Method:

_____
_____
_____
_____
_____
_____
_____
_____
_____
_____
_____
_____

Suitable for freezing: Y / N

Calories per serving:

Difficulty?

1   2   3   4   5

How healthy?

1   2   3   4   5

Date first made:

Notes:

Taste test:

Recipe:

5

Ingredients:

_____   _____
_____   _____
_____   _____
_____   _____

Method:

_____
_____
_____
_____
_____
_____
_____
_____
_____
_____

Serves:

⏲ Preparation time:

⏲ Cooking time:

Suitable for freezing: Y / N

Calories per serving:

Difficulty?
1 2 3 4 5

How healthy?
1 2 3 4 5

Date first made:

Notes:

Taste test:

Recipe:

6

Ingredients:

_____   _____
_____   _____
_____   _____
_____   _____
_____   _____

Method:

_____
_____
_____
_____
_____
_____
_____
_____
_____
_____
_____
_____

Notes:

Serves:

🕐 Preparation time:

🕐 Cooking time:

Suitable for freezing: Y / N

Calories per serving:

Difficulty?
1 2 3 4 5

How healthy?
1 2 3 4 5

Date first made:

Taste test:

Recipe:

7

Ingredients:

Method:

Serves:

Preparation time:

Cooking time:

Suitable for freezing: Y / N

Calories per serving:

Difficulty?
1 2 3 4 5

How healthy?
1 2 3 4 5

Date first made:

Notes:

Taste test:

Recipe:

8

Ingredients:

Method:

Notes:

Serves:

🕐 Preparation time:

🕐 Cooking time:

Suitable for freezing: Y / N

Calories per serving:

Difficulty?
1 2 3 4 5

How healthy?
1 2 3 4 5

Date first made:

Taste test:

Recipe:

9

Ingredients:

Method:

Notes:

Serves:

🕐 Preparation time:

🕐 Cooking time:

Suitable for freezing: Y / N

Calories per serving:

Difficulty?

1 2 3 4 5

How healthy?

1 2 3 4 5

Date first made:

Taste test:

Recipe:

10

Ingredients:

Method:

Notes:

Serves:

⏱ Preparation time:

⏱ Cooking time:

Suitable for freezing: Y / N

Calories per serving:

Difficulty?
1 2 3 4 5

How healthy?
1 2 3 4 5

Date first made:

Taste test:

Recipe:

11

Ingredients:

_____   _____
_____   _____
_____   _____
_____   _____

Method:

_____
_____
_____
_____
_____
_____
_____
_____
_____
_____
_____
_____

Notes:

Serves:

🕐 **Preparation time:**

🕐 **Cooking time:**

Suitable for freezing: Y / N

Calories per serving:

Difficulty?
1   2   3   4   5

How healthy?
1   2   3   4   5

Date first made:

Taste test:
👍   👌   👎

Recipe:

12

Ingredients:

Method:

Notes:

Serves:

🕐 Preparation time:

🕐 Cooking time:

Suitable for freezing: Y / N

Calories per serving:

Difficulty?

1   2   3   4   5

How healthy?

1   2   3   4   5

Date first made:

Taste test:

Recipe:

13

Ingredients:

Method:

Notes:

Serves:

Preparation time:

Cooking time:

Suitable for freezing: Y / N

Calories per serving:

Difficulty?

1 2 3 4 5

How healthy?

1 2 3 4 5

Date first made:

Taste test:

Recipe:

14

Ingredients:

Method:

Notes:

Serves:

Preparation time:

Cooking time:

Suitable for freezing: Y / N

Calories per serving:

Difficulty?

1 2 3 4 5

How healthy?

1 2 3 4 5

Date first made:

Taste test:

Recipe:

15

Ingredients:

Method:

Notes:

Serves:

🕐 Preparation time:

🕐 Cooking time:

Suitable for freezing: Y / N

Calories per serving:

Difficulty?

1 2 3 4 5

How healthy?

1 2 3 4 5

Date first made:

Taste test:

Recipe:

16

Ingredients:

_____   _____
_____   _____
_____   _____
_____   _____
_____   _____

Method:

_____
_____
_____
_____
_____
_____
_____
_____
_____
_____
_____
_____

Serves:

⏲ Preparation time:

⏲ Cooking time:

Suitable for freezing: Y / N

Calories per serving:

Difficulty?

1   2   3   4   5

How healthy?

1   2   3   4   5

Date first made:

Notes:

Taste test:

Recipe:

17

Ingredients:

Method:

Serves:

🕐 **Preparation time:**

🕐 **Cooking time:**

Suitable for freezing: Y / N

Calories per serving:

Difficulty?
1 2 3 4 5

How healthy?
1 2 3 4 5

Date first made:

Notes:

Taste test:

Recipe:

18

Ingredients:

_____   _____
_____   _____
_____   _____
_____   _____
_____   _____

Method:

_____
_____
_____
_____
_____
_____
_____
_____
_____
_____
_____
_____
_____

Notes:

Serves:

🕐 Preparation time:

🕐 Cooking time:

Suitable for freezing: Y / N

Calories per serving:

Difficulty?

1 2 3 4 5

How healthy?

1 2 3 4 5

Date first made:

Taste test:

Recipe:

19

Ingredients:

Serves:

⏱ Preparation time:

⏱ Cooking time:

Method:

Suitable for freezing: Y / N

Calories per serving:

Difficulty?

1   2   3   4   5

How healthy?

1   2   3   4   5

Date first made:

Notes:

Taste test:

Recipe:

20

Ingredients:

Method:

Notes:

Serves:

Preparation time:

Cooking time:

Suitable for freezing: Y / N

Calories per serving:

Difficulty?
1   2   3   4   5

How healthy?
1   2   3   4   5

Date first made:

Taste test:

Recipe:

21

Ingredients:

Method:

Notes:

Serves:

🕐 Preparation time:

🕐 Cooking time:

Suitable for freezing: Y / N

Calories per serving:

Difficulty?
1   2   3   4   5

How healthy?
1   2   3   4   5

Date first made:

Taste test:

Recipe:

22

Ingredients:

Method:

Notes:

Serves:

Preparation time:

Cooking time:

Suitable for freezing: Y / N

Calories per serving:

Difficulty?
1   2   3   4   5

How healthy?
1   2   3   4   5

Date first made:

Taste test:

Recipe:

23

Ingredients:

Serves:

⏱ Preparation time:

⏱ Cooking time:

Method:

Suitable for freezing: Y / N

Calories per serving:

Difficulty?

1   2   3   4   5

How healthy?

1   2   3   4   5

Date first made:

Notes:

Taste test:

Recipe:

24

Ingredients:

_____   _____
_____   _____
_____   _____
_____   _____
_____   _____

Method:

_____
_____
_____
_____
_____
_____
_____
_____
_____
_____
_____
_____

Notes:

Serves:

🕐 Preparation time:

🕐 Cooking time:

Suitable for freezing: Y / N

Calories per serving:

Difficulty?
1 2 3 4 5

How healthy?
1 2 3 4 5

Date first made:

Taste test:

Recipe:

25

Ingredients:

Method:

Notes:

Serves:

⏲ Preparation time:

⏲ Cooking time:

Suitable for freezing: Y / N

Calories per serving:

Difficulty?
1   2   3   4   5

How healthy?
1   2   3   4   5

Date first made:

Taste test:

Recipe:

26

Ingredients:

_____ _____
_____ _____
_____ _____
_____ _____
_____ _____

Method:

_____
_____
_____
_____
_____
_____
_____
_____
_____
_____
_____
_____
_____

Notes:

Serves:

🕐 Preparation time:

🕐 Cooking time:

Suitable for freezing: Y / N

Calories per serving:

Difficulty?
1 2 3 4 5

How healthy?
1 2 3 4 5

Date first made:

Taste test:

Recipe:

27

Ingredients:

_____   _____
_____   _____
_____   _____
_____   _____
_____   _____

Method:

_____
_____
_____
_____
_____
_____
_____
_____
_____
_____
_____
_____

Serves:

🕐 Preparation time:

🕐 Cooking time:

Suitable for freezing: Y / N

Calories per serving:

Difficulty?
1   2   3   4   5

How healthy?
1   2   3   4   5

Date first made:

Taste test:

Notes:

Recipe:

28

Ingredients:

Method:

Serves:

🕐 Preparation time:

🕐 Cooking time:

Suitable for freezing: Y / N

Calories per serving:

Difficulty?

1   2   3   4   5

How healthy?

1   2   3   4   5

Date first made:

Notes:

Taste test:

Recipe:

29

Ingredients:

Method:

Serves:

Preparation time:

Cooking time:

Suitable for freezing: Y / N

Calories per serving:

Difficulty?
1   2   3   4   5

How healthy?
1   2   3   4   5

Date first made:

Notes:

Taste test:

Recipe:

30

Ingredients:

Method:

Notes:

Serves:

🕐 Preparation time:

🕐 Cooking time:

Suitable for freezing: Y / N

Calories per serving:

Difficulty?

1   2   3   4   5

How healthy?

1   2   3   4   5

Date first made:

Taste test:

Recipe:

31

Ingredients:

_____ _____
_____ _____
_____ _____
_____ _____

Method:

_____
_____
_____
_____
_____
_____
_____
_____
_____
_____
_____
_____

Notes:

Serves:

Preparation time:

Cooking time:

Suitable for freezing: Y / N

Calories per serving:

Difficulty?

1   2   3   4   5

How healthy?

1   2   3   4   5

Date first made:

Taste test:

Recipe:

32

Ingredients:

_____ _____
_____ _____
_____ _____
_____ _____
_____ _____

Method:

_____
_____
_____
_____
_____
_____
_____
_____
_____
_____
_____
_____
_____

Notes:

Serves:

Preparation time:

Cooking time:

Suitable for freezing: Y / N

Calories per serving:

Difficulty?
1   2   3   4   5

How healthy?
1   2   3   4   5

Date first made:

Taste test:

Recipe:

33

Ingredients:

Method:

Notes:

Serves:

⏲ Preparation time:

⏲ Cooking time:

Suitable for freezing: Y / N

Calories per serving:

Difficulty?
1 2 3 4 5

How healthy?
1 2 3 4 5

Date first made:

Taste test:

Recipe:

34

Ingredients:

_____   _____
_____   _____
_____   _____
_____   _____
_____   _____

Method:

_____
_____
_____
_____
_____
_____
_____
_____
_____
_____
_____
_____
_____
_____

Notes:

Serves:

Preparation time:

Cooking time:

Suitable for freezing: Y / N

Calories per serving:

Difficulty?

1 2 3 4 5

How healthy?

1 2 3 4 5

Date first made:

Taste test:

Recipe:

35

Ingredients:

Method:

Notes:

Serves:

⏱ Preparation time:

⏱ Cooking time:

Suitable for freezing: Y / N

Calories per serving:

Difficulty?

1 2 3 4 5

How healthy?

1 2 3 4 5

Date first made:

Taste test:

Recipe:

36

Ingredients:

_____   _____
_____   _____
_____   _____
_____   _____

Method:

_____
_____
_____
_____
_____
_____
_____
_____
_____
_____
_____
_____

Notes:

Serves:

Preparation time:

Cooking time:

Suitable for freezing: Y / N

Calories per serving:

Difficulty?
1   2   3   4   5

How healthy?
1   2   3   4   5

Date first made:

Taste test:

Recipe:

37

Ingredients:

Method:

Notes:

Serves:

⏱ Preparation time:

⏱ Cooking time:

Suitable for freezing: Y / N

Calories per serving:

Difficulty?
1 2 3 4 5

How healthy?
1 2 3 4 5

Date first made:

Taste test:

Recipe:

38

Ingredients:

-- --
-- --
-- --
-- --

Method:

Serves:

🕐 Preparation time:

🕐 Cooking time:

Suitable for freezing: Y / N

Calories per serving:

Difficulty?

1 2 3 4 5

How healthy?

1 2 3 4 5

Date first made:

Notes:

Taste test:

Recipe:

39

Ingredients:

Method:

Notes:

Serves:

⏱ Preparation time:

⏱ Cooking time:

Suitable for freezing: Y / N

Calories per serving:

Difficulty?
1 2 3 4 5

How healthy?
1 2 3 4 5

Date first made:

Taste test:

Recipe:

Ingredients:

Method:

Notes:

40

Serves:

⏰ Preparation time:

⏰ Cooking time:

Suitable for freezing: Y / N

Calories per serving:

Difficulty?
1   2   3   4   5

How healthy?
1   2   3   4   5

Date first made:

Taste test:

Recipe:

41

Ingredients:

Method:

Notes:

Serves:

Preparation time:

Cooking time:

Suitable for freezing: Y / N

Calories per serving:

Difficulty?

1   2   3   4   5

How healthy?

1   2   3   4   5

Date first made:

Taste test:

Recipe:

42

Ingredients:

Method:

Notes:

Serves:

Preparation time:

Cooking time:

Suitable for freezing: Y / N

Calories per serving:

Difficulty?
1 2 3 4 5

How healthy?
1 2 3 4 5

Date first made:

Taste test:

Recipe:

43

Ingredients:

Method:

Notes:

Serves:

Preparation time:

Cooking time:

Suitable for freezing: Y / N

Calories per serving:

Difficulty?

1   2   3   4   5

How healthy?

1   2   3   4   5

Date first made:

Taste test:

Recipe:

44

Ingredients:

Method:

Serves:

Preparation time:

Cooking time:

Suitable for freezing: Y / N

Calories per serving:

Difficulty?

1 2 3 4 5

How healthy?

1 2 3 4 5

Date first made:

Notes:

Taste test:

Recipe:

45

Ingredients:

_____   _____
_____   _____
_____   _____
_____   _____

Method:

Serves:

⏰ Preparation time:

⏰ Cooking time:

Suitable for freezing: Y / N

Calories per serving:

Difficulty?
1   2   3   4   5

How healthy?
1   2   3   4   5

Date first made:

Notes:

Taste test:

Recipe:

46

Ingredients:

Method:

Notes:

Serves:

Preparation time:

Cooking time:

Suitable for freezing: Y / N

Calories per serving:

Difficulty?

1 2 3 4 5

How healthy?

1 2 3 4 5

Date first made:

Taste test:

Recipe:

47

Ingredients:

_____   _____
_____   _____
_____   _____
_____   _____

Method:

_____
_____
_____
_____
_____
_____
_____
_____
_____
_____
_____
_____
_____

Serves:

🕐 Preparation time:

🕐 Cooking time:

Suitable for freezing: Y / N

Calories per serving:

Difficulty?
1   2   3   4   5

How healthy?
1   2   3   4   5

Date first made:

Notes:

Taste test:

Recipe:

48

Ingredients:

Method:

Serves:

🕐 Preparation time:

🕐 Cooking time:

Suitable for freezing: Y / N

Calories per serving:

Difficulty?

1   2   3   4   5

How healthy?

1   2   3   4   5

Date first made:

Notes:

Taste test:

Recipe:

49

Ingredients:

Method:

Notes:

Serves:

Preparation time:

Cooking time:

Suitable for freezing: Y / N

Calories per serving:

Difficulty?
1   2   3   4   5

How healthy?
1   2   3   4   5

Date first made:

Taste test:

Recipe:

50

Ingredients:

--------------------------------- ---------------------------------
--------------------------------- ---------------------------------
--------------------------------- ---------------------------------
--------------------------------- ---------------------------------
--------------------------------- ---------------------------------

Method:

Serves:

⏲ Preparation time:

⏲ Cooking time:

Suitable for freezing: Y / N

Calories per serving:

Difficulty?

1   2   3   4   5

How healthy?

1   2   3   4   5

Date first made:

Notes:

Taste test:

Recipe:

51

Ingredients:

Serves:

⏱ Preparation time:

⏱ Cooking time:

Method:

Suitable for freezing: Y / N

Calories per serving:

Difficulty?

1 2 3 4 5

How healthy?

1 2 3 4 5

Date first made:

Notes:

Taste test:

Recipe:

52

Ingredients:

------------------------------------   ------------------------------------
------------------------------------   ------------------------------------
------------------------------------   ------------------------------------
------------------------------------   ------------------------------------
----

Method:

Notes:

Serves:

🕐 Preparation time:

🕐 Cooking time:

Suitable for freezing: Y / N

Calories per serving:

Difficulty?

1   2   3   4   5

How healthy?

1   2   3   4   5

Date first made:

Taste test:

Recipe:

53

Ingredients:

Method:

Notes:

Serves:

🕐 Preparation time:

🕐 Cooking time:

Suitable for freezing: Y / N

Calories per serving:

Difficulty?

1   2   3   4   5

How healthy?

1   2   3   4   5

Date first made:

Taste test:

Recipe:

54

Ingredients:

---------------------------------   ---------------------------------
---------------------------------   ---------------------------------
---------------------------------   ---------------------------------
---------------------------------   ---------------------------------

Method:

Notes:

Serves:

Preparation time:

Cooking time:

Suitable for freezing: Y / N

Calories per serving:

Difficulty?

1   2   3   4   5

How healthy?

1   2   3   4   5

Date first made:

Taste test:

Recipe:

55

Ingredients:

_____   _____
_____   _____
_____   _____
_____   _____

Method:

_____
_____
_____
_____
_____
_____
_____
_____
_____
_____
_____
_____
_____

Notes:

Serves:

Preparation time:

Cooking time:

Suitable for freezing: Y / N

Calories per serving:

Difficulty?
1   2   3   4   5

How healthy?
1   2   3   4   5

Date first made:

Taste test:

Recipe:

56

Ingredients:

------------------------------ ------------------------------
------------------------------ ------------------------------
------------------------------ ------------------------------
------------------------------ ------------------------------
----

Method:

Serves:

Preparation time:

Cooking time:

Suitable for freezing: Y / N

Calories per serving:

Difficulty?
1 2 3 4 5

How healthy?
1 2 3 4 5

Date first made:

Notes:

Taste test:

Recipe:

57

Ingredients:

Method:

Notes:

Serves:

🕐 Preparation time:

🕐 Cooking time:

Suitable for freezing: Y / N

Calories per serving:

Difficulty?

1   2   3   4   5

How healthy?

1   2   3   4   5

Date first made:

Taste test:

Recipe:

58

Ingredients:

Method:

Notes:

Serves:

Preparation time:

Cooking time:

Suitable for freezing: Y / N

Calories per serving:

Difficulty?

1 2 3 4 5

How healthy?

1 2 3 4 5

Date first made:

Taste test:

Recipe:

59

Ingredients:

Method:

Notes:

Serves:

⏰ Preparation time:

⏰ Cooking time:

Suitable for freezing: Y / N

Calories per serving:

Difficulty?
1 2 3 4 5

How healthy?
1 2 3 4 5

Date first made:

Taste test:

Recipe:

60

Ingredients:

Method:

Notes:

Serves:

🕐 Preparation time:

🕐 Cooking time:

Suitable for freezing: Y / N

Calories per serving:

Difficulty?
1   2   3   4   5

How healthy?
1   2   3   4   5

Date first made:

Taste test:

Recipe:

61

Ingredients:

Method:

Notes:

Serves:

Preparation time:

Cooking time:

Suitable for freezing: Y / N

Calories per serving:

Difficulty?

1 2 3 4 5

How healthy?

1 2 3 4 5

Date first made:

Taste test:

Recipe:

62

Ingredients:

Method:

Notes:

Serves:

Preparation time:

Cooking time:

Suitable for freezing: Y / N

Calories per serving:

Difficulty?
1 2 3 4 5

How healthy?
1 2 3 4 5

Date first made:

Taste test:

Recipe:

63

Ingredients:

Method:

Serves:

Preparation time:

Cooking time:

Suitable for freezing: Y / N

Calories per serving:

Difficulty?
1 2 3 4 5

How healthy?
1 2 3 4 5

Date first made:

Notes:

Taste test:

Recipe:

64

Ingredients:

Method:

Notes:

Serves:

Preparation time:

Cooking time:

Suitable for freezing: Y / N

Calories per serving:

Difficulty?
1 2 3 4 5

How healthy?
1 2 3 4 5

Date first made:

Taste test:

Recipe:

65

Ingredients:

Method:

Notes:

Serves:

🕐 Preparation time:

🕐 Cooking time:

Suitable for freezing: Y / N

Calories per serving:

Difficulty?

1 2 3 4 5

How healthy?

1 2 3 4 5

Date first made:

Taste test:

Recipe:

66

Ingredients:

Method:

Serves:

⏱ Preparation time:

⏱ Cooking time:

Suitable for freezing: Y / N

Calories per serving:

Difficulty?
1 2 3 4 5

How healthy?
1 2 3 4 5

Date first made:

Notes:

Taste test:

Recipe:

67

Ingredients:

Method:

Notes:

Serves:

🕐 Preparation time:

🕐 Cooking time:

Suitable for freezing: Y / N

Calories per serving:

Difficulty?

1   2   3   4   5

How healthy?

1   2   3   4   5

Date first made:

Taste test:

Recipe:

68

Ingredients:

------------------------------   ------------------------------
------------------------------   ------------------------------
------------------------------   ------------------------------
------------------------------   ------------------------------
----

Method:

Notes:

Serves:

🕐 Preparation time:

🕐 Cooking time:

Suitable for freezing: Y / N

Calories per serving:

Difficulty?

1 2 3 4 5

How healthy?

1 2 3 4 5

Date first made:

Taste test:

Recipe:

69

Ingredients:

Method:

Notes:

Serves:

🕐 Preparation time:

🕐 Cooking time:

Suitable for freezing: Y / N

Calories per serving:

Difficulty?

1 2 3 4 5

How healthy?

1 2 3 4 5

Date first made:

Taste test:

Recipe:

70

Ingredients:

Serves:

⏰ Preparation time:

⏰ Cooking time:

Method:

Suitable for freezing: Y / N

Calories per serving:

Difficulty?

1   2   3   4   5

How healthy?

1   2   3   4   5

Date first made:

Notes:

Taste test:

Recipe:

71

Ingredients:

Method:

Notes:

Serves:

Preparation time:

Cooking time:

Suitable for freezing: Y / N

Calories per serving:

Difficulty?

1 2 3 4 5

How healthy?

1 2 3 4 5

Date first made:

Taste test:

Recipe:

72

Ingredients:

Method:

Serves:

⏱ Preparation time:

⏱ Cooking time:

Suitable for freezing: Y / N

Calories per serving:

Difficulty?

1 2 3 4 5

How healthy?

1 2 3 4 5

Date first made:

Notes:

Taste test:

Recipe:

73

Ingredients:

_____   _____
_____   _____
_____   _____
_____   _____

Method:

_____
_____
_____
_____
_____
_____
_____
_____
_____
_____
_____

Serves:

Preparation time:

Cooking time:

Suitable for freezing: Y / N

Calories per serving:

Difficulty?
1   2   3   4   5

How healthy?
1   2   3   4   5

Date first made:

Notes:

Taste test:

Recipe:

74

Ingredients:

------------------------   ------------------------
------------------------   ------------------------
------------------------   ------------------------
------------------------   ------------------------

Method:

Notes:

Serves:

⏲ **Preparation time:**

⏲ **Cooking time:**

Suitable for freezing: Y / N

Calories per serving:

Difficulty?
1   2   3   4   5

How healthy?
1   2   3   4   5

Date first made:

Taste test:
👍   👌   👎

Recipe:

75

Ingredients:

Method:

Notes:

Serves:

Preparation time:

Cooking time:

Suitable for freezing: Y / N

Calories per serving:

Difficulty?
1   2   3   4   5

How healthy?
1   2   3   4   5

Date first made:

Taste test:

Recipe:

76

Ingredients:

_____ _____
_____ _____
_____ _____
_____ _____

Method:

_____
_____
_____
_____
_____
_____
_____
_____
_____
_____
_____

Notes:

Serves:

Preparation time:

Cooking time:

Suitable for freezing: Y / N

Calories per serving:

Difficulty?
1   2   3   4   5

How healthy?
1   2   3   4   5

Date first made:

Taste test:

Recipe:

77

Ingredients:

Method:

Notes:

Serves:

🕐 **Preparation time:**

🕐 **Cooking time:**

Suitable for freezing: Y / N

Calories per serving:

Difficulty?
1 2 3 4 5

How healthy?
1 2 3 4 5

Date first made:

Taste test:

Recipe:

78

Ingredients:

_____   _____
_____   _____
_____   _____
_____   _____
_____

Method:

_____
_____
_____
_____
_____
_____
_____
_____
_____
_____
_____
_____

Notes:

Serves:

⏲ Preparation time:

⏲ Cooking time:

Suitable for freezing: Y / N

Calories per serving:

Difficulty?

1   2   3   4   5

How healthy?

1   2   3   4   5

Date first made:

Taste test:

Recipe:

79

Ingredients:

Method:

Notes:

Serves:

Preparation time:

Cooking time:

Suitable for freezing: Y / N

Calories per serving:

Difficulty?

1   2   3   4   5

How healthy?

1   2   3   4   5

Date first made:

Taste test:

Recipe:

80

Ingredients:

------------------------------   ------------------------------
------------------------------   ------------------------------
------------------------------   ------------------------------
------------------------------   ------------------------------
------------------------------   ------------------------------

Method:

Notes:

Serves:

🕐 Preparation time:

🕐 Cooking time:

Suitable for freezing: Y / N

Calories per serving:

Difficulty?
1   2   3   4   5

How healthy?
1   2   3   4   5

Date first made:

Taste test:

Recipe:

81

Ingredients:

_____   _____
_____   _____
_____   _____
_____   _____
_____   _____

Method:

_____
_____
_____
_____
_____
_____
_____
_____
_____
_____
_____
_____

Notes:

Serves:

Preparation time:

Cooking time:

Suitable for freezing: Y / N

Calories per serving:

Difficulty?
1   2   3   4   5

How healthy?
1   2   3   4   5

Date first made:

Taste test:

Recipe:

82

Ingredients:

Method:

Notes:

Serves:

🕐 Preparation time:

🕐 Cooking time:

Suitable for freezing: Y / N

Calories per serving:

Difficulty?

1   2   3   4   5

How healthy?

1   2   3   4   5

Date first made:

Taste test:

Recipe:

83

Ingredients:

Method:

Notes:

Serves:

🕐 Preparation time:

🕐 Cooking time:

Suitable for freezing: Y / N

Calories per serving:

Difficulty?

1   2   3   4   5

How healthy?

1   2   3   4   5

Date first made:

Taste test:

Recipe:

84

Ingredients:

------------------------------   ------------------------------

------------------------------   ------------------------------

------------------------------   ------------------------------

------------------------------   ------------------------------

Method:

Serves:

⏱ Preparation time:

⏱ Cooking time:

Suitable for freezing: Y / N

Calories per serving:

Difficulty?

1   2   3   4   5

How healthy?

1   2   3   4   5

Date first made:

Notes:

Taste test:

Recipe:

85

Ingredients:

Method:

Notes:

Serves:

⏱ Preparation time:

⏱ Cooking time:

Suitable for freezing: Y / N

Calories per serving:

Difficulty?
1 2 3 4 5

How healthy?
1 2 3 4 5

Date first made:

Taste test:

Recipe:

86

Ingredients:

Method:

Serves:

🕐 Preparation time:

🕐 Cooking time:

Suitable for freezing: Y / N

Calories per serving:

Difficulty?

1 2 3 4 5

How healthy?

1 2 3 4 5

Date first made:

Notes:

Taste test:

Recipe:

87

Ingredients:

Method:

Notes:

Serves:

🕐 Preparation time:

🕐 Cooking time:

Suitable for freezing: Y / N

Calories per serving:

Difficulty?

1 2 3 4 5

How healthy?

1 2 3 4 5

Date first made:

Taste test:

Recipe:

88

Ingredients:

Method:

Notes:

Serves:

⏱ Preparation time:

⏱ Cooking time:

Suitable for freezing: Y / N

Calories per serving:

Difficulty?

1　2　3　4　5

How healthy?

1　2　3　4　5

Date first made:

Taste test:

Recipe:

89

Ingredients:

Serves:

⏱ Preparation time:

⏱ Cooking time:

Method:

Suitable for freezing: Y / N

Calories per serving:

Difficulty?

1   2   3   4   5

How healthy?

1   2   3   4   5

Date first made:

Notes:

Taste test:

Recipe:

90

Ingredients:

Method:

Notes:

Serves:

⏱ Preparation time:

⏱ Cooking time:

Suitable for freezing: Y / N

Calories per serving:

Difficulty?
1 2 3 4 5

How healthy?
1 2 3 4 5

Date first made:

Taste test:

Recipe:

91

Ingredients:

Method:

Notes:

Serves:

🕐 Preparation time:

🕐 Cooking time:

Suitable for freezing: Y / N

Calories per serving:

Difficulty?

1　2　3　4　5

How healthy?

1　2　3　4　5

Date first made:

Taste test:

Recipe:

92

Ingredients:

_____   _____
_____   _____
_____   _____
_____   _____
_____

Method:

_____
_____
_____
_____
_____
_____
_____
_____
_____
_____
_____
_____
_____

Notes:

Serves:

⏲ Preparation time:

⏲ Cooking time:

Suitable for freezing: Y / N

Calories per serving:

Difficulty?

1   2   3   4   5

How healthy?

1   2   3   4   5

Date first made:

Taste test:

Recipe:

93

Ingredients:

Method:

Notes:

Serves:

🕐 Preparation time:

🕐 Cooking time:

Suitable for freezing: Y / N

Calories per serving:

Difficulty?

1 2 3 4 5

How healthy?

1 2 3 4 5

Date first made:

Taste test:

Recipe:

94

Ingredients:

Method:

Serves:

🕐 Preparation time:

🕐 Cooking time:

Suitable for freezing: Y / N

Calories per serving:

Difficulty?

1 2 3 4 5

How healthy?

1 2 3 4 5

Date first made:

Notes:

Taste test:

Recipe:

95

Ingredients:

Method:

Notes:

Serves:

🕐 Preparation time:

🕐 Cooking time:

Suitable for freezing: Y / N

Calories per serving:

Difficulty?
1 2 3 4 5

How healthy?
1 2 3 4 5

Date first made:

Taste test:

Recipe:

96

Ingredients:

Method:

Notes:

Serves:

Preparation time:

Cooking time:

Suitable for freezing: Y / N

Calories per serving:

Difficulty?
1 2 3 4 5

How healthy?
1 2 3 4 5

Date first made:

Taste test:

Recipe:

97

Ingredients:

Method:

Notes:

Serves:

Preparation time:

Cooking time:

Suitable for freezing: Y / N

Calories per serving:

Difficulty?
1 2 3 4 5

How healthy?
1 2 3 4 5

Date first made:

Taste test:

Recipe:

98

Ingredients:

Method:

Serves:

⏱ **Preparation time:**

⏱ **Cooking time:**

Suitable for freezing: Y / N

Calories per serving:

Difficulty?
1   2   3   4   5

How healthy?
1   2   3   4   5

Date first made:

Notes:

Taste test:

Recipe:

99

Ingredients:

Method:

Serves:

🕐 Preparation time:

🕐 Cooking time:

Suitable for freezing: Y / N

Calories per serving:

Difficulty?

1 2 3 4 5

How healthy?

1 2 3 4 5

Date first made:

Notes:

Taste test:

Recipe:

100

Ingredients:

------------------------------ ------------------------------
------------------------------ ------------------------------
------------------------------ ------------------------------
------------------------------ ------------------------------
----

Method:

Serves:

🕐 Preparation time:

🕐 Cooking time:

Suitable for freezing: Y / N

Calories per serving:

Difficulty?
1   2   3   4   5

How healthy?
1   2   3   4   5

Date first made:

Notes:

Taste test:
👍   👌   👎

Printed in Great Britain
by Amazon